The Diary of
Sam Watkins,
a Confederate Soldier

Edited by Ruth Ashby
Illustrations and map by Laszlo Kubinyi

BENCHMARK BOOKS

MARSHALL CAVENDISH
NEW YORK

Benchmark Books
Marshall Cavendish
99 White Plains Road
Tarrytown, New York 10591-9001
www.marshallcavendish.com

Library of Congress Cataloging-in-Publication Data

Watkins, Samuel R. (Samuel Rush)
  [Co. Aytch, or, A side show of the big show and other sketches.
Selections]
  The diary of Sam Watkins, a Confederate soldier / edited by Ruth Ashby.
    p. cm. — (In my own words)
Selections from the author's Co. Aytch, or, A side show of the big show and other sketches,
originally published: Nashville, Tenn. : Cumberland Presbyterian Pub. House, 1882.
  ISBN 0-7614-1646-3
  1. Watkins, Samuel R. (Samuel Rush)—Juvenile literature. 2. Confederate States of
America. Army. Tennessee Infantry Regiment, 1st. Company H—Juvenile literature. 3.
United States—History—Civil War, 1861–1865—Personal narratives, Confederate—
Juvenile literature. 4. Tennessee—History—Civil War, 1861–1865—Personal narratives—
Juvenile literature. 5. United States—History—Civil War, 1861–1865—Regimental histo-
ries—Juvenile literature. 6. Tennessee—History—Civil War, 1861–1865—Regimental
histories—Juvenile literature. 7. Soldiers—Tennessee—Biography—Juvenile literature.
[1. Watkins, Samuel R. (Samuel Rush) 2. Confederate States of America. Army.
Tennessee Infantry Regiment, 1st. Company H. 3. United States—History—Civil War,
1861–1865—Personal narratives, Confederate. 4. United States—History—Civil War,
1861–1865—Regimental histories. 5. Tennessee—History—Civil War, 1861–1865. 6.
Soldiers. 7. Diaries.] I. Ashby, Ruth. II. Title. III. Series.
  E579.51st .W36 2004
  973.7'468—dc21

                              2003001478

Photo of Sam Watkins courtesy of the Franklin Fulton Collection, used by permission of
Mrs. Ruth McAlister of Columbia, Tennessee.

Series design by Adam Mietlowski

Printed in China

1 3 5 6 4 2

To my nephew, Stephen Gutz

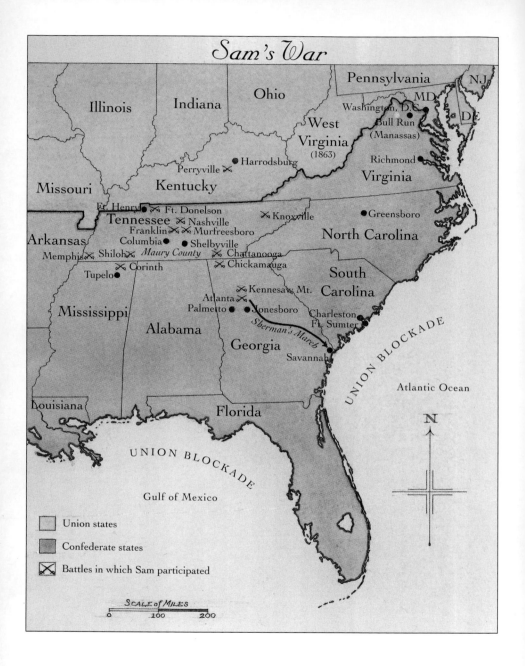

Sam's War

Illinois

Indiana

Ohio

Pennsylvania

N.J.

MD

DE

Washington, D.C.

West
Virginia
(1863)

Bull Run
(Manassas)

Richmond ●

Virginia

● Harrodsburg

Perryville ✗

Kentucky

Missouri

● Greensboro

✗ Knoxville

Ft. Henry ● ✗ Ft. Donelson

Tennessee ✗ Nashville

Franklin ✗✗ Murfreesboro

North Carolina

Arkansas

Columbia ● ● Shelbyville

Memphis ✗ ✗ Shiloh *Maury County* ✗ Chattanooga

✗ Corinth

✗ Chickamauga

South
Carolina

Tupelo ●

✗ Kennesaw Mt.

Mississippi

Atlanta ✗

Palmetto ● ● Jonesboro

Charleston ●
Ft. Sumter ●

Alabama

Sherman's March

Georgia

Savannah ●

UNION BLOCKADE

Atlantic Ocean

Louisiana

Florida

N

UNION BLOCKADE

Gulf of Mexico

☐ Union states

▨ Confederate states

✗ Battles in which Sam participated

SCALE of MILES

0   100   200

Sam's Book

Introduction

In April 1861 Samuel Rush Watkins enlisted as a private in the Confederate Army. Only twenty-one years old, he was bold, idealistic, and eager to defend his native state against the Union Army. He expected a brief, glorious war. Neither he nor the others who enlisted with him could possibly have foreseen the four years of hardship and slaughter that would follow.

Watkins was born on June 26, 1839, on a farm near Columbia, Tennessee. He worked for a while as a clerk in a general store before going to Jackson College in Columbia. While Sam studied Latin, theology, and rhetoric, the United States moved to the brink of civil war. The issue of slavery had threatened to tear the country apart for decades. The South depended on the labor of black slaves to produce the cotton, tobacco, and rice that were the basis of its economic system. The North had a more varied and highly industrialized economy. Not dependent on forced agricultural labor, it gradually outlawed slavery.

Things came to a head with the presidential election of 1860. Republicans who wanted to limit slavery's expansion into the Western territories—or abolish it altogether—challenged the pro-slavery Democrats.

Sam in his Company H uniform

When Republican Abraham Lincoln won the election, many Southerners feared that their economy and way of life would be ruined. In December 1860 South Carolina became the first state to secede, or separate, from the Union. It was followed by Alabama, Florida, Georgia, Louisiana, Mississippi, Texas, Virginia, North Carolina, Tennessee, and Arkansas. The rebellious states formed a new nation, the Confederate States of America, and elected a president, Jefferson Davis.

Why did Sam Watkins become a Confederate soldier? He does not seem to have held strong beliefs on the issue of slavery, and he owned no slaves himself. He fought not to defend slavery, but to defend Tennessee. Watkins believed in the principle of states' rights. Each state, he thought, had the authority to say no to the Federal government. In other words, Tennessee had the right to uphold slavery or not, as it chose—and the right to secede from the United States when it wanted to. Even twenty years later, Watkins could still write, "I am as firm in my convictions today of the right of secession as I was in 1861."

Watkins and his neighbors in Maury County formed Company H of the First Tennessee Infantry Regiment. Company H would fight some of the toughest battles of the war, including Shiloh, Perryville, Chattanooga, Chickamauga, the Hundred Days' Battles, and the campaigns of Atlanta, Franklin, and Nashville. Even though Watkins was wounded three times, at Murfreesboro, Atlanta, and

Nashville, his injuries were never life-threatening. His comrades, though, died by the thousands. Of the 3,200 men enlisted in the First Tennessee Regiment, only 125 survived. And of the original 120 members of Company H, only 7 made it back home to Maury County. Sam Watkins was one of them.

After the final surrender of Confederate troops in April 1865, Watkins married his childhood sweetheart, Virginia Jane Mayes, "Jennie." He settled down with her to raise eight children and run a farm and a general store. Sixteen years later, he was finally ready to tell about what he had witnessed. In 1881 Watkins began to submit articles about his war experience to his local newspaper. The following year the pieces were gathered into a book: *"Co. Aytch," Maury Grays, First Tennessee Regiment; or, A Side Show of the Big Show.* More than one hundred years later, *Co. Aytch* (Company H) has become one of the best known and best loved personal accounts of the Civil War.

As Watkins likes to remind his readers, he was but a "humble private" in the army infantry. Being a common foot soldier enabled him to see the absurdity, the suffering, and the heroism of war, from the endless marches and the ceaseless quest for food, to the pandemonium of battle and the bravery of ordinary men. His memoirs are often funny, sometimes painful, and always moving. Watkins is a natural storyteller, and it's easy to get caught up in the drama of his story. You'll thrill at his narrow escapes from the Yankees, laugh at his contest with a stubborn mule, and shudder at the death of his best friend. By the time you are finished, you'll know a lot about what it was really like to be a "humble private" in the Civil War. You'll also learn to admire Sam Watkins, who shows us how a soldier could keep his humanity and sense of humor even in the midst of terror and death.

Here, then, is Sam Watkins in his own words.

—Ruth Ashby
Huntington, New York

A Side Show of the Big Show:
The experiences of Sam Watkins,
a humble private,
in the Civil War

April 14, 1861, vs. April 14, 1882

In these memoirs, after the lapse of twenty years, we propose to fight our battles o'er again.

There is nothing that so much delights the old soldier as to revisit the scenes and battlefields with which he was once so familiar. In these pages I do not pretend to write the history of the war. I only give a few sketches and incidents that came under the observation of a simple private in the rear ranks of the Rebel army.

Histories all tell of great achievements of great men, who wear the laurels of victory and have high positions in civil life. But in the following pages I propose to tell of the fellows who did the shooting and killing, the fortifying and ditching, the sweeping of the streets, the drilling, the standing guard. They drew eleven dollars per month and rations, and also drew the ramrod and tore the cartridge. Pardon me if I use the pronoun "I" too frequently. I do not wish to be called egotistical. I only write of what I saw as a humble private in an infantry regiment, commonly called a "webfoot." I write entirely from memory. You must remember, kind reader, that these things happened twenty years ago, and twenty years is a long time in the life of any individual.

I was twenty-one years old then, and at that time I was not married. Now I have a house full of young "rebels," clustering around my knees and bumping against my elbow, as I write these reminiscences of the war of secession.

Did you live in that stormy period? Do you remember those stirring times, in the year of our Lord eighteen hundred and sixty-one? Fort Sumter was fired upon from Charleston by troops under General Beauregard, and Major Anderson, of the Federal army, surrendered. The die was cast; war was declared. Tennessee, loyal to her Southern sister states, passed the ordinance of secession, and enlisted under the Stars and Bars.

From that day on, every person was almost eager for the war, and we were all afraid it would be over and we not in the fight. Companies were made up, regiments organized. Everywhere could be seen Southern cockades made by our ladies and our sweethearts. Rousing speeches would fairly make our hair stand on end with intense patriotism, and we wanted to march right off and whip twenty Yankees.

After being drilled and disciplined at Camp Cheatham, we learned of the advance of McClellan's army into Virginia, toward Harper's Ferry and Bull Run.

The Federal army was advancing all along the line. They expected to march right into the heart of the South, set the negroes free, take our property, and whip the Rebels back into the Union. But they found the people of the South in earnest.

Secession may have been wrong in the abstract, and has been tried and settled by the sword and the bayonet. But I am as firm in my convictions today of the right of

FORT SUMTER

The Civil War officially began on a spring day in 1861. At 4:30 A.M. on April 12, Confederate troops fired on the Federal-held Fort Sumter in Charleston Harbor, South Carolina. After four thousand rounds of shot had been poured into the fort, Major Robert Anderson was forced to surrender to Confederate general P. G. T. Beauregard. At the surrender ceremony, a powder keg accidentally exploded and killed Union private Daniel Hough. He was the first soldier to die in the war. More than 600,000 deaths were to come.

secession as I was in 1861. The South is our country, the North is the country of those who live there. We are an agricultural people; they are a manufacturing people. They are the descendants of the good old Puritan Plymouth Rock stock, and we of the South from the proud and aristocratic stock of cavaliers. We believe in the doctrine of state rights, and they in the doctrine of centralization.

To Virginia

The vote of the regiment was taken, and we all voted to go to Virginia. The Southern Confederacy had established its capital at Richmond. A long line of box-cars was drawn up at Camp Cheatham one morning in July. The bugle sounded to strike tents and to place everything on board the cars. Every soldier had enough blankets, shirts, pants, and old boots to last a year. The empty bottles and jugs would have set up a first-class drugstore. In addition, every one of us had his gun, cartridge-box, knapsack, and three days' rations, a pistol on each side and a long Bowie knife. We got in and on top of the box-cars, the whistle sounded, and amid the waving of hats, handkerchiefs, and flags, we bid a long farewell and forever to old Camp Cheatham.

We went bowling along twenty or thirty miles an hour, as fast as steam could carry us. At every town and station citizens and ladies were waving their handkerchiefs and hurrahing for Jeff Davis and the Southern Confederacy. Magnificent banquets were prepared for us all along the entire route.

But the Yankees were advancing on Manassas. July 21st found us a hundred miles from that fierce day's battle. That night, after the battle was fought and won, our train drew up at Manassas Junction.

Magnificent banquets were prepared for us all along the entire route.

Everyone was wild, nay, frenzied with the excitement of victory. We felt that the war was over, and we would have to return home without even seeing a Yankee soldier. How we envied those that were wounded. We thought at that time that we would have given a thousand dollars to have been in the battle, and to have had our arm shot off, so that we could have returned home with an empty sleeve.

From Manassas our train moved on to Staunton, Virginia, [and Millboro]. From there we had to foot it. We went over the Allegheny Mountains.

I was on every march that was ever made by the First Tennessee Regiment during the whole war, and at this time I cannot remember a harder or more fatiguing march. It seemed that mountain was piled upon mountain. From the foot to the top of the mountain the soldiers lined the road, broken down and exhausted. First one blanket was thrown away, and then another. Now and then a good pair of pants, old boots and shoes, Sunday hats, pistols, and Bowie knives strewed the road. Old bottles and jugs, and various and sundry articles were lying pell-mell everywhere. Up and up, and onward and upward we pulled and toiled, until we reached the very top. There burst upon our view one of the grandest and most beautiful landscapes we ever beheld.

Nestled in the valley right before us was Bath Alum and Warm Springs. It seemed to me at that time, a glimpse of a better and brighter world beyond. A glad shout arose from those who had gained the top, which encouraged the others to persevere. At last we got to Warm Springs. Here

THE BATTLE OF BULL RUN

A day after the fall of Fort Sumter, Abraham Lincoln and Jefferson Davis both called up troops and prepared for war. Thousands of men from across the North swarmed into Washington, D.C., to begin their training. Just across the Potomac River from the Capitol, Confederate troops began to gather in Virginia. Both sides were convinced the war would be short — a matter of a few months, at most. Bowing to public pressure, Lincoln approved an immediate attack on the enemy in Virginia.

On July 21, 1861, Federal troops met the Confederates on the shores of a little creek called Bull Run in the town of Manassas. Much to the North's surprise, the Rebels whipped the Union troops. Inexperienced soldiers on both sides were shocked by the blood, smoke, and noise of actual battle. Suddenly, everyone realized this would be a real war after all.

they had a nice warm dinner waiting for us. The second day after leaving Warm Springs we came to Big Springs.

One evening, General Robert E. Lee came to our camp. He was a fine-looking gentleman, and wore a mustache. He was dressed in blue cottonade and looked like some good boy's grandpa. I felt like going up to him and saying good evening, Uncle Bob! I remember going up mighty close and sitting there and listening to his conversation with the officers of our regiment. He had a calm and collected air about him, his voice was kind and tender, and his eye was as gentle as a dove's. His whole person, looks, and manner had a kind of gentle and soothing magnetism that drew every one to him and made them love, respect, and honor him. When I saw that he was getting ready to start I ran and caught his horse and led him up to him. Lee took the reins of the bridle in his hand and said, "Thank you, my son," and rode off. My heart went with him.

From this time forward, we were ever on the march —*tramp, tramp, tramp.* Lee's corps, Stonewall Jackson's division—I refer you to the histories for the marches made by these commanders in the first year of the war. Well, we followed them.

One morning the main body of the regiment was marching leisurely along the road, when *bang, debang, debang, bang.* We had marched into a Yankee ambuscade [ambush].

All at once everything was a scene of consternation and confusion. We did not know whether to run or stand, when Captain Field gave the command to fire and charge the bushes. We charged the bushes and saw the Yankees running through them, and fired on them as they retreated. I do not know how many Yankees were killed, if any. Our company (H) had one man killed.

After the fighting was over, where, oh where was all the fine rigging on our officers? It could not be seen. Corporals, Sergeants, Lieutenants, Captains, all had torn all the fine lace of their clothing. I asked several of them why they had torn the insignia of their rank, and they always answered, "Humph. You think that I was going to be a target for the Yankees to shoot at?"

You see, this was our first battle. The officers had not found out that minnie as well as cannon balls were blind. They thought that the balls would hunt for them and not hurt the privates. I always shot at privates. It was they that did the shooting and killing, and if I could kill or wound a private, why, my chances were so much the better. I always looked upon officers as harmless personages. I always tried to kill those that were trying to kill me.

One night I stood picket guard on the Potomac with a detail of the Third Arkansas Regiment. I had to stand all night. The snow came pelting down as large as goose eggs. About midnight, the snow ceased to fall, and became quiet. While I was peering through the darkness, my eyes suddenly fell upon the outlines of a man. The more I looked, the more I was convinced that it was a Yankee picket. I could see his hat and coat—yes, see his gun. What was I to do? The relief was several hundred yards in the rear. At last a cold sweat broke out all over my body. Turkey bumps rose. I summoned all the nerves and bravery that I could command and said, "Halt! Who goes there?"

There being no response, I became resolute. I marched right up to it and stuck my bayonet through and through it. It was a stump.

It was with sorrow and regret that we bade farewell to Old Virginia's shore to go to other fields of carnage and death. Away back yonder, in good old Tennessee, our homes and loved ones were being robbed and insulted, our fields laid waste, our cities sacked. Duty as well as patriotism called us back to our native home, to try and defend it. Virginia, we bid you a long farewell!

Shiloh

This was the first big battle in which our regiment had ever been engaged. The First Tennessee was the advance guard on Saturday evening, and we did a little skirmishing.

On Sunday morning, a clear, beautiful, and still day, the order was given for the whole army to advance, and to attack immediately. We were supporting an Alabama brigade. The fire opened — *bang, bang, bang a rattle de bang, a boom, de bang, boom, bang, boom whirr-siz-siz-siz* — a ripping, roaring, boom, bang! The air was full of balls and deadly missiles.

As we were advancing to support the Alabama brigade in our front, it gave way and began running wildly through our lines, routed and seemingly stricken in fear. Some of the boys of our regiment would laugh at them and ask what they were running for, and would commence to say *"Flicker! Flicker! Flicker!"* like the bird called the yellowhammer. Advancing a little further on, we saw General Albert Sidney Johnston surrounded by his staff. We saw some little commotion among those who surrounded him, but we did not know at the time that he was dead. The fact was kept from the troops.

About noon a courier dashed up and ordered us to go

A BLOODY BATTLE

One of the Union goals in the war was to secure control of the vital rivers that fed the South: the Cumberland, the Tennessee, the Ohio, and the Mississippi. In spring 1862 Union General Ulysses S. Grant was systematically advancing along the Tennessee. After capturing the important river posts of Fort Henry and Fort Donelson, he made camp at Pittsburg Landing, Tennessee, near a Methodist meeting house named Shiloh Church. There the Confederates under Albert Sidney Johnston attacked on Sunday morning, April 6, 1862. In the first twelve hours of the battle, jubilant Confederates pushed the Federals back almost to the river. General Johnston was shot in the leg and bled to death before medical help arrived.

That night the Union Army was reinforced, and Monday morning Grant sprang back. By the afternoon it was the Confederates who were forced to retreat.

Shiloh was a very narrow victory for the North. Both sides were appalled by the carnage. Union casualties were 13,000 men dead, wounded, and missing, and Confederate casualties were 9,500. At the time Shiloh was the bloodiest battle ever fought in North America.

forward and support General Bragg's center. We had to pass over the ground where troops had been fighting all day.

I had heard and read of battlefields, of horses and men, of cannons and wagons, all jumbled together, while the ground was strewn with dead and dying and wounded. But I must confess I never realized the "pomp and circumstance" of the thing called glorious war until I saw this. Men were lying in every conceivable position; the dead lying with their eyes wide open, the wounded begging piteously for help, and some waving their hats and shouting to us to go forward. It all seemed to me a dream. I seemed to be in a sort of haze, when *siz, siz, siz,* the minnie balls from the Yankee line began to whistle around our ears.

Down would drop first one fellow and then another, either killed or wounded, when we were ordered to charge bayonets. When the order to charge was given, I got happy. It was fun then. We were crowding them. One more charge, then their lines wavered and broke. They retreated in wild confusion. We were jubilant; we were triumphant.

When in the very midst of our victory, there came an order to halt. What! Halt after today's victory? The word *halt* turned victory into defeat.

The soldiers had passed through the Yankee camps and saw all the good things that they had to eat in their sutler's store and officers' marquees [tents]. It was but a short time before every soldier was rummaging to see what he could find. The boys were in clover.

This was Sunday.

On Monday the tide was reversed.

Now, those Yankees were whipped, fairly whipped, and according to all the rules of war they ought to have retreated. But they didn't. Buell's army, by forced marches, had come to Grant's assistance at the eleventh hour.

Gun-boats and transports were busily crossing Buell's army all of Sunday night. We could hear their boats ringing their bells and hear the puff of smoke and steam from their boilers.

We made a good fight on Monday morning, and I was taken by surprise when the order came for us to retreat instead of advance. But a private soldier is but an automaton, and knows nothing of what is going on among the generals. I am only giving the chronicles of little things and events that came under my own observation. Should you desire to find out more about the battle, I refer you to history.

On Monday morning I captured a mule. He was not a fast mule, and I soon found out that he thought he knew as much as I did. All the bombasting [shouting] that I could give him would not make him accelerate his speed. If I wanted him to go on one side of the road he was sure to be possessed of an equal desire to go on the other side.

Finally I and my mule fell out. I got a big hickory stick and began to flail him over the head, but he would only shake his head and flop his ears and seem to say,

"Well, now, you think you are smart, don't you?"

Me and mule worried along until we came to a creek. Mule did not desire to cross. But the caisson* of a battery was about to cross. The driver said, "I'll take your mule over for you." So he got a large rope, tied one end around the mule's neck and the other to the caisson, and ordered the driver to whip up. The rope was stronger than the mule's "no," and he was finally prevailed upon by the strength of the rope to cross the creek.

I got on him again, when all of a sudden, he lifted his head, pricked up his ears, got a little faster, and finally broke into a gallop and then a run. I could not stop him until Corinth, Mississippi.

Well, [in Corinth,] here we were again "reorganizing." After a big battle, which always disorganizes an army, what wonder is it that some men had to be shot, merely for discipline's sake? And what wonder that General Bragg's name became a terror to deserters and evil doers? Men were shot by scores.

Soldiers had enlisted for twelve months only. Now the terms for which they had enlisted had expired, and they naturally looked upon it that they had a right to go home. They wanted to see their families, in fact, wanted to go home anyhow. War had become a reality; they were tired of it. A law had been passed by the Confederate Congress called the Conscript Act. A soldier had no right

*caisson — vehicle that carries artillery ammunition

I got on him again, when all of a sudden, he lifted his head, pricked up his ears, broke into a gallop, and then a run. I could not stop him until Corinth, Mississippi.

to volunteer and to choose the branch of service he preferred. He was conscripted.

From this time on till the end of the war, a soldier was simply a machine, a conscript. It was mighty rough on Rebels. We cursed the war, we cursed Bragg, we cursed the Southern Confederacy. All our pride and valor had gone, and we were sick of war and the Southern Confederacy.

Another law was made by the Confederate Congress about this time, allowing every person who owned twenty negroes to go home. It gave us the blues; we wanted twenty negroes. There was raised the howl of "rich man's war, poor man's fight."

They were deserting by the thousands. When men were to be shot or whipped, the whole army was marched to the horrid scene to see a poor trembling wretch tied to a post and a platoon of twelve men drawn up in line to put him to death. The hushed command of "Ready, aim, fire!" would make the conscript loathe the very name of Southern Confederacy.

None of General Bragg's soldiers ever loved him. He was looked upon as a merciless tyrant. The soldiers were very scantily fed. Bragg never was a good feeder, and rations with us were always scarce. We became starved skeletons; naked and ragged Rebels. The chronic diarrhea became the scourge of the army. The camp became one vast hospital.

We went into summer quarters at Tupelo. Our principal

GENERALS OF THE ARMY OF TENNESSEE

The ill-starred Confederate Army of Tennessee went through no fewer than five commanding generals during the Civil War.

- The first, the promising Albert Sidney Johnston, died an untimely death at Shiloh.

- Then came P. G. T. Beauregard, who was relieved of command by President Jefferson Davis just a few weeks later.

- The crabby Braxton Bragg was hated by the ordinary soldier. Although he had a number of victories, Davis blamed him for the loss of Chattanooga and replaced him with Joseph Johnston.

- Johnston was a superb strategic commander and popular with the troops. His orders were to keep Atlanta from being captured, but he kept falling back instead of attacking. In spite of the Confederate success at Kennesaw Mountain, Davis had him removed.

- The tragic John Bell Hood lost his right leg at Chickamauga and the use of an arm at Gettysburg. Although he was a courageous fighter, he lacked the strategic skills necessary to lead an army. Under his command the army lost Atlanta and was very nearly wiped out at Nashville. After Hood resigned in winter 1865, Davis had no choice but to reinstate Johnston. It was Johnston who finally had to surrender the Army of Tennessee on April 26, 1865.

occupation at this place was playing poker, chuck-a-luck, and cracking graybacks (lice). Every soldier had a brigade of lice on him. At first the boys would go off in the woods and hide to louse themselves, but that was unnecessary. The ground fairly crawled with lice.

The boys would frequently have a louse race. There was one fellow who was winning all the money; his lice would run quicker and crawl faster than anybody's lice. We could not understand it. The lice were placed in plates—this was the race course—and the first that crawled off was the winner. At last we found out D's trick: he always heated his plate.

Kentucky

After the troops had recovered their health and spirits at Tupelo, we made an advance into Kentucky. I remember how gladly the citizens of Kentucky received us. They had the prettiest girls that God ever made. They could not do too much for us. They had heaps and stacks of cooked rations along our route, with wine and cider everywhere, and the glad shouts of "Hurrah for our Southern boys!" greeted and welcomed us at every house.

Ah, the boys felt like soldiers again. They could fight now. It was the same old proud soldier of yore. The bands played "Dixie" and "Bonnie Blue Flag," the citizens cheered, and the ladies waved their handkerchiefs and threw us bouquets.

The good time we were having was too good to last. We were at Harrodsburg; the Yankees were approaching Perryville under General Buell. When we marched to Perryville, we marched the whole night long. We, the private soldiers, did not know what was going on among the generals. All that we had to do was march, march, march.

I was in every battle, skirmish, and march that was made by the First Tennessee Regiment during the war, and I do not remember a harder contest or more evenly fought battle than that of Perryville on October 8, 1862. Both sides claimed the victory — both were whipped.

I stood picket guard in Perryville the night before the battle—a Yankee on one side of the street, and I on the other. We got very friendly during the night, and made a raid on a citizen's pantry, where we captured a bucket of honey, a pitcher of sweet milk, and three or four biscuits. The old citizen was not at home—he and his whole household had gone visiting, I believe. In fact, I think all of the citizens of Perryville were taken with a sudden notion of visiting about this time.

At length the morning dawned. Our line was drawn up on one side of Perryville, the Yankee army on the other. The blue coats lined the hillside in plain view. You could count the number of their regiments by the number of their flags. We could see the huge war dogs [cannons] frowning at us, ready at any moment to belch forth their fire and smoke.

Never on earth were our troops more eager for the engagement to open. The Yankees commenced to march toward their left, and we marched almost parallel to our right—both sides watching each other's maneuvers and movements. About 12 o'clock, as we were marching through a cornfield, they opened their war dogs upon us.

The battle now opened in earnest. From one end of the line to the other it seemed to be a solid sheet of blazing smoke and fire. Two lines of battle confronted us. We killed almost everyone in the first line, and were soon charging over the second. Right in our immediate front was their third and main line of battle, from which four Napoleon guns poured their deadly fire.

We did not recoil. But our line was hurled back by the leaden hail that was poured into our very faces. Eight color-bearers were killed at one discharge of their cannon. We were right up among the very wheels of their Napoleon guns. It was death now to retreat to either side. We were soon in a hand-to-hand fight—every man for himself— using the butts of our guns and bayonets. Such obstinate fighting I never had seen before or since.

The iron storm passed through our ranks, mangling and tearing men to pieces. The very air seemed full of stifling smoke and fire, which seemed the very pit of hell. It was a life to life and death to death grapple. The sun was poised above us, a great red ball, sinking slowly in the west. Yet the scene of battle and carnage continued.

The mantle of night fell upon the scene. I do not know which side whipped.* But I know I helped to bring off those four Napoleon guns that night.

The battle of Perryville presented a strange scene. The dead, dying, and wounded of both armies, Confederate and Federal, were blended in inextricable confusion. I helped bring off our wounded that night. We worked the whole night. The next morning about daylight a wounded comrade, Sam Campbell, complained of being cold, and asked me to lie down beside him. I did so, and was soon asleep. When I awoke the poor fellow was stiff

*The Yankees succeeded in driving the Rebels from Kentucky.

and cold in death. His spirit had flown to its home beyond the skies.

From Perryville we went to Camp Dick Robinson and [then to Cumberland Gap]. Along the route it was nothing but *tramp, tramp, tramp.* The same monotonous tramp, tramp, tramp up hill and down hill, through long and dusty lands, weary, worn out and hungry. I have seen soldiers fast asleep, and no doubt dreaming of home and loved ones there, as they staggered along in their places in the ranks. I know that on many a weary night's march I have slept, and slept soundly, while marching along in my proper place. Sometimes, when weary, broken down, and worn out, some member of the regiment would start a tune, and every man would join in.

After a while we would see the morning star rise in the east, and then after a while, the sun would begin to shoot his slender rays athwart [across] the eastern sky. The boys would wake up and begin laughing and talking as if they had just risen from a good feather bed, and were perfectly refreshed and happy. We would usually stop at some stream or other about breakfast time, and all wash our hands and faces and eat breakfast, if we had any, and then commence our weary march again. If we were halted for one minute, every soldier would drop down, and resting on his knapsack, would go to sleep.

We marched on. The scene of a few days ago came unbidden to my mind. Where were many of my old friends and comrades? They lay yonder at Perryville, unburied, on the field of battle. They lay where they fell. More than three hundred and fifty members of my regiment, the First Tennessee, numbered among the killed and wounded.

They left their homes, families, and loved ones a little more than twelve months ago, dressed in their gay uniforms. They lay yonder. No friendly hands ever closed their eyes in death. No kind, gentle, and loving mother was there to shed a tear over and say farewell to their darling boy. No sister's gentle touch ever wiped the death damp from off their dying brows. Noble boys, brave boys! They willingly gave their lives to their country's cause.

Soldiers, comrades, friends, noble boys, farewell! We will meet no more on earth, but up yonder some day we will have a grand reunion.

Murfreesboro

We came from Knoxville to Chattanooga, and seemed destined to make a permanent stay there. We remained for several months, but soon we were on the tramp again.

From Chattanooga, Bragg's army went to Murfreesboro. I was on picket duty at the time the advance was made by Rosecrans [a Union general]. I had orders to allow no one to pass. But while standing at my post, a horseman rode up behind me. He advanced up, and pulling a piece of paper out of his pocket, handed it to me to read. It was an order from General Leonidas Polk [a Confederate general] to allow the bearer to pass. I read it, and when I looked up to hand it back to him, he had a pistol cocked and leveled in my face.

Says he, "Drop that gun, you're my prisoner." I knew if I resisted he would shoot me. I dropped the gun.

I did not wish to spend my winter in a Northern prison. What was worse, I would be called a deserter from my post of duty.

The Yankee picket lines were not a half mile off. I was perfectly willing to let the spy go on his way rejoicing—for such he was—but he wanted to capture a Rebel.

Finally says I, "Let's play quits. I think you are a soldier; you look like a gentleman. I am a picket; you know the

"Drop that gun, you're my prisoner."

responsibility resting on me. You go your way and leave me here. Is it a bargain?"

Says he, "I would not trust a Secesh* on his word, oath, or bond. March, I say."

I quickly made up my mind. My gun was at my feet, and one step would get it. I made a quick glance over my shoulder, and grabbed at my gun. He divined [guessed] my motive, and fired. The ball missed its aim. He put spurs to his horse, but I pulled him down. I did not capture the spy, though I captured his horse, bridle, and saddle.

The next day, the Yankees were found out to be advancing. We were ordered forward to the attack. We were right upon the Yankee line on the Wilkerson turnpike in Murfreesboro. The Yankees were shooting our men down by scores. I continued to load and shoot, until a fragment of a shell struck me on the arm. And then a minnie ball passed through the same, paralyzed my arm, and wounded and disabled me.

When I went back to the field hospital, I overtook another man walking along. I remember first noticing that his left arm was entirely gone. His face was white as a sheet. He was walking along, when all at once he dropped down and died without a struggle, or a groan. I could tell of hundreds of such incidents of the battlefield, but tell only this one, because I remember it so distinctly.

At Shelbyville, Duck River wended its way to Columbia [Watkins's hometown]. Andy Wilson and I

*Secesh —secessionist; Confederate

thought that we would slip off and go down the river in a canoe. We had not gone far before the thing capsized, and we swam ashore. But we were outside of the lines now, and without passes. So we put our sand paddles [feet] to work and landed in Columbia that night. I loved a maid, and so did Andy. When I went to see my sweetheart that night I asked her to pray for me, because I thought the prayers of a pretty woman would go a great deal further "up yonder" than mine would. I also met cousin Alice at my father's front gate, and told her that she must pray for me, because I knew I would be court-martialed as soon as I got back. I had no idea of deserting the army and only wanted to see the maid that I loved.

When I got back to Shelbyville, I was arrested and carried to the guard-house and sentenced to thirty days' fatigue duty and to forfeit four months' pay at eleven dollars per month.

But fortunately for me, General Leonidas Polk had issued an order that very day promising pardon to all soldiers absent without leave if they would return. I got the guard to march me up to his headquarters and told him of my predicament, and he ordered my release, but said nothing of remitting the fine. So when we were paid off at Chattanooga I was left out. The Confederate States of America was richer by forty-four dollars.

Chattanooga and Chickamauga

Rosecrans' army was in motion. The Federals were advancing, but as yet they were afar off. Chattanooga must be fortified.

About this time my father paid me a visit. Rations were mighty scarce. I was glad to see him, but ashamed to let him know how poorly off for something to eat we were. We were living on parched corn. I thought of a happy plan to get him a good dinner. So I asked him to let us go up to the Colonel's tent.

Says I, "Colonel Field, I desire to introduce you to my father, and as rations are a little short in my mess, I thought you might have a little better, and could give him a good dinner."

"Yes," says Colonel Field, "I will be glad to divide my rations with him. Also, I would like you to stay and take dinner with me."

About this time a young African, Whit, came in with a frying-pan of parched corn and dumped it on an old oil cloth and said, "Master, dinner is ready." That was all the Colonel had. He was living like ourselves—on parched corn.

We continued to fortify and build breastworks at Chattanooga.

The Tennessee River is about a quarter of a mile wide at Chattanooga. Right across the river was an immense

FOOD

The Civil War soldier was always hungry. Even in the Union Army, where supplies were more plentiful, men mostly relied on staples such as hard biscuits, called hardtack. Confederate soldiers had it worse, right from the beginning. The Union blockade of the Southern coastline prevented most ships from reaching port, so the South suffered shortages in food, clothing, and other necessities. Union seizure of farmland and destruction of railroad lines meant that little food could be harvested or delivered to market. As a result, by the end of the war both Southern soldiers and civilians were on the verge of starvation.

Instead of hardtack, Confederate soldiers subsisted on corn bread. One soldier recalled, "The corn bread would get so hard and moldy that when we broke it, it looked like it had cobwebs in it." Other staples included coffee, bacon, and salt pork. Only rarely were troops issued fresh fruits, vegetables, or meat. The meat they did get was usually rancid and crawling with maggots. No wonder armies on the march sometimes scavenged what they could from the countryside—corn, "goober peas" (peanuts), even chickens or pigs from neighboring farms. For most of the war Johnny Reb was malnourished, dreaming of the good food at home.

cornfield. The green corn was waving with every little breeze that passed, and everything seemed to say, "Come hither, Johnny Reb." The river was wide, but we were hungry. We pulled off our clothes and launched into the turbid stream, and were soon on the other bank. Here was the field, and here were the roasting-ears; but where was the raft or canoe?

Well, what was to be done? We began to shuck the corn. We would pull up a few shucks on one ear, and tie it to the shucks of another, until we had at least a hundred tied together. We put the train of corn into the river, and as it began to float off we jumped in. Taking the foremost ear in our mouth, we struck out for the other bank. Well, we made the landing all correct.

One morning while sitting around our campfires we heard a boom, and a bomb shell passed over our heads. The Yankee army was right on the other bank of the Tennessee River. Bragg did not know of their approach until the cannon fired.

Wagons were packed, camps were broken up, and there was a general hubbub everywhere. But your old soldier is always ready at a moment's notice. We left Chattanooga, but whither bound we knew not, and cared not. We marched toward Chickamauga Creek and camped on the banks on Friday night.

On Saturday morning we commenced to cross over. No sooner had we crossed than an order came to double quick. General Forrest's [a Confederate general] cavalry had opened the battle. We held our position for two hours and ten minutes in the midst of deadly fire, when General Forrest galloped up and said, "Look out, you are almost surrounded. You had better fall back."

The big battle was fought the next day, Sunday. The morning of that September day, the sun rose over the eastern hills clear and beautiful. The day itself seemed to have a Sabbath-day look about it. The battlefield was in a rough and broken country, with trees and under-growth. It looked wild, weird, uncivilized.

Our corps (Polk's) being in the engagement the day before, we were held in reserve. Reader, were you ever held in reserve of an attacking army? All that could demoralize, and I may say intimidate a soldier was being enacted, and he was not allowed to participate. We were moved from one position to another, but always under fire. Our nerves were strung to their utmost tension.

Finally General Leonidas Polk rode up and turned to General Cheatham. "General, move your division and attack at once."

General Cheatham says, "Forward boys, and give 'em h__l."

We raised one long, cheering shout and charged right upon their breastworks. They were pouring their deadly missiles into our advancing ranks. We did not stop to look around to see who was killed and wounded,

CHICKAMAUGA

An important gateway to the South, Chattanooga, Tennessee, was a major Union target in summer 1863. Union general William Rosecrans forced the Army of Tennessee to evacuate Chattanooga by posting his men on hills and mountains around the city. Then he went after the retreating army, now posted near Chickamauga Creek in northern Georgia.

Unbeknown to Rosecrans, the Confederates had been reinforced and now outnumbered the Federals by ten thousand men. In the ensuing Battle of Chickamauga on September 19–20, the successful Confederate troops forced the Union Army to retreat back to Chattanooga.

Even though this was a major Confederate victory, little was gained. As Watkins points out, the Union Army still held Chattanooga —the point of all the fighting. And the cost of the battle was horrendous, with more than 18,500 Confederate and 16,000 Union casualties.

but pressed right up their breastworks, and planted our battle-flag upon it. They wavered and broke and ran in every direction.

We remained upon the battlefield of Chickamauga all night. Everything had fallen into our hands. We captured a great many prisoners and small arms, and many pieces of artillery and wagons and provisions. The Confederate and Federal dead, wounded, and dying were everywhere, scattered over the battlefield. Men were lying where they fell, shot in every conceivable part of the body. Some with their entrails torn out and still hanging to them. Some with their under jaw torn off. Some with both eyes shot out, with one eye hanging down on their cheek. In fact you might walk over the battlefield and find men shot from the crown of the head to the tip end of the toe. And then to see all those dead, wounded, and dying horses, with their heads and tails drooping. I felt like shedding a tear for those innocent dumb brutes.

Reader, a battlefield, after the battle, is a sad and sorrowful sight to look at.

One scene I now remember. While a detail of us were passing over the field with a dim lantern, looking for our wounded soldiers to carry to the hospital, we came across a group of ladies, looking among the killed and wounded for their relatives. One of the ladies screamed out, "Oh, there he is! Poor fellow! Dead, dead, dead!"

"Dead, dead, dead!"

She ran to the pile of slain and raised the dead man's head and placed it on her lap. She began kissing him and saying, "Oh, oh, they have killed my darling, my darling! Oh, mother, mother, what must I do! Oh, they have killed him!"

I could witness the scene no longer. I turned and walked away. William A. Hughes was crying and remarked, "Oh, law me, this war is a terrible thing."

After retreating from Chickamauga, the Yankees attempted to re-form their broken lines. We advanced to attack them, but they soon fell back to Chattanooga. We knew they were in an impregnable position. We had built those breastworks and forts, and knew whereof we spoke.

A few weeks later, in late November, the armies met again. At the Battle of Missionary Ridge, a height south of the city of Chattanooga, the whole Confederate Army was routed. It was the first defeat our army had ever suffered. We retreated, and went into winter quarters at Ringgold Gap and Dalton, Tennessee.

Hundred Days' Battles

General Joseph E. Johnston now took command of the army. General Bragg was relieved and had become Jeff Davis's war advisor at Richmond, Virginia. We had followed General Bragg all through this long war. We had got sorter used to his ways, but he was never popular with his troops. I felt sorry for him.

But now let me introduce you to old Joe. Fancy, if you please, a man about fifty years old, rather small of stature, but firmly and compactly built. He had an open and honest countenance and a keen but restless black eye that seemed to read your very inmost thoughts. He found the army depleted by battles and worse, by desertion. The morale of the army was gone. The spirit of the soldiers was crushed, their hope gone. They would not answer at roll call. A feeling of mistrust pervaded the whole army.

When the news came that General Joe E. Johnston had taken command of the Army of Tennessee, men returned to their companies, and order was restored. He issued a universal amnesty to all soldiers absent without leave. He ordered two days' rations to be issued. He ordered sugar and coffee and flour to be issued instead of blue beef. He ordered new tents, new suits of clothes, shoes, and hats. There had been a revolution, sure enough.

He allowed us what General Bragg had never allowed mortal man—a furlough. A new era had dawned. He was loved, respected, admired; yea almost worshipped by his troops. I don't believe there was a soldier in his army but would gladly have died for him. Old Joe had greater military insight than any general of the South, not excepting even Lee.

We went into winter quarters at Dalton, and remained there during the cold, bad winter of 1863–64, about four months. The usual routine of army life was carried on day by day, with not many incidents to vary the monotony. But occasionally the soldiers would engage in a snow ball battle, in which generals, colonels, captains, and privates all took part. The snow balls would begin to fly hither and thither, with an occasional knock down, and sometimes an ugly wound, where some mean fellow had enclosed a rock in his snow ball. It was fun while it lasted. But after it was over the soldiers were wet, cold, and uncomfortable.

One day, a party of us privates concluded we would go across the Canasauga River on a raid. After traveling for some time, we saw a neat-looking farmhouse, and sent one of the party forward to reconnoiter. He returned in a few minutes and announced that he had found a fine fat sow in a pen near the house. Now, the plan we formed was for two of us to go into the house and keep the inmates interested and the other was to drive off the hog.

I was one of the party which went into the house. There was no one there but an old lady and her sick and

CAMP LIFE

The Civil War was a seasonal war, fought mainly in the spring, summer, and fall. Long periods of time were spent in camp, where soldiers drilled, repaired equipment, and readied themselves for the next big fight. But they had some free time, too, especially in the winter months when the weather made training difficult. To ward off boredom, the men found various ways to amuse themselves. One soldier in the Army of Tennessee wrote, "We had a few books, a set of chess men, took one daily paper, and kept on hand a supply of writing materials. We became expert in making loaf bread and telling yarns."

Making music was a favorite pastime on both sides. Every camp had its brass bands, choruses, and even amateur theaters. Soldiers enjoyed singing together around the campfires at night. Other occupations, though, weren't quite so innocent: cockfighting, for instance, or gambling. Soldiers would bet on almost anything: cards, board and dice games, wrestling matches, or baseball. In Sam Watkins's company, they even bet on lice races.

Camps were often so unsanitary, and the food was so bad, that men by the thousands fell ill of disease: dysentery, typhoid fever, and infectious diseases such as measles and chicken pox. It is estimated that four times as many men died of illness during the war as of wounds from the battlefield.

widowed daughter. They invited us in very pleasantly and kindly, and soon prepared us a very nice and good dinner. The old lady told us of all her troubles and trials. Her husband had died before the war, and she had three sons in the army, two of whom had been killed, and the youngest, who had been conscripted, was taken with the camp fever and died in the hospital at Atlanta. She had nothing to subsist on, after eating up what they then had. I soon went out, having made up my mind to have nothing to do with the hog affair. I did not know how to act. I was in a bad fix. I had heard the gun fire and knew its portent. I knew the hog was dead. I went up the road and on looking back I saw the old lady coming and screaming at the top of her voice, "You got my hog!"

I had a guilty conscience, I assure you. The hog was cooked, but I did not eat a piece of it.

A short time afterward an old citizen from Maury County visited me. My father sent me, by him, a silver watch—which I am wearing today—and eight hundred dollars in Confederate money. I took one hundred dollars and went back by my lone self to the old lady's house.

I helped the old lady catch a chicken (an old hen—about the last she had), for dinner, went with her in the garden and pulled a bunch of eschalots, brought two buckets of water, and cut and brought enough wood to last several days.

After a while, she invited me to dinner. After dinner I sat down by her side, took her old hand in mine, and told her the whole affair of the hog, from beginning to end. I asked her as a special act of kindness and favor to me, to take the hundred dollars. I laid the money on the table and left. I have never in my life made a raid upon anybody else.

I went on a furlough. When I got back to Dalton, I found the Yankee army advancing; they were at Rocky Face Ridge. From then on it was battle, battle, battle every day for one hundred days.

Today, April 14, 1882, I say, and honestly say, that I sincerely believe the combined forces of the whole Yankee nation could never have broken General Joseph E. Johnston's line of battle, beginning at Rocky Face Ridge and ending on the banks of the Chattahoochee.

One day our orderly Sergeant informed me that it was my regular time to go on duty. I reported to the proper place, and we were taken to the headquarters of General Leonidas Polk. We had to go over into the enemy's lines, and make such observations as we could, and report back by daylight in the morning. You may be sure my heart beat like a muffled drum when I heard our orders.

I felt like making my will. But I tried to whistle to keep my spirits up. We followed the relief guard, and one by one stepped off from the rear. We found ourselves between the picket lines of the two armies. Fortune seemed to favor us. It was getting dusky twilight, and we saw the relief guard of the Yankees just putting on their picket. I walked on as if I was just relieved. I had passed their lines, when I turned back. Says I, "Captain, what guard is this?"

"Nien bocht, you bet," was what I understood him to say.

I had run across the detail of a Dutch [German-speaking] regiment.* I passed on. I finally got over their breastworks. I was fearful I would run into some camp or headquarter guard, and the countersign would be demanded of me. But I thought of the way that I had gotten it hundreds of times before in our army.

I saw a courier come out of his tent, get on his horse, and ride toward where I stood. As he approached, says I, "Halt! Who goes there?"

"A friend with the countersign."

He advanced and whispered in my ear the word *United*. He rode on. I had gotten their countersign, and felt I was no longer a prisoner. I went all over their camp, and met and talked with a great many soldiers, but could get no information from them.

About 3 o'clock I heard the assembly sound. I knew then that it was about time for me to be getting out of the way. I got back into our lines, and reported to General Polk.

He was killed that very day on the Kennesaw line.

*German immigrants in the Union Army formed German-speaking regiments in Ohio, Pennsylvania, New York, Wisconsin, and other states.

The Dead Angle

The First and Twenty-seventh Tennessee Regiments will ever remember the battle of Dead Angle, which was fought June 27, 1864, on the Kennesaw line, near Marietta, Georgia. It was one of the hottest and longest days of the year, and one of the most desperate battles fought during the whole war. Our regiment was stationed on an angle, a little spur of the mountain. It seemed fun for the guns of the whole Yankee army to play upon this point. We would work hard every night to strengthen our breastworks, and the very next day they would be torn down smooth with the ground by solid shots and shells from the guns of the enemy.

Well, on the fateful morning of June 27th, the sun rose clear and cloudless. The heavens seemed made of brass, and the earth of iron. All of a sudden, our pickets jumped into our works and reported the Yankees advancing. Almost at the same time, a solid line of blue coats came up the hill. My pen is unable to describe the scene of carnage and death that ensued in the next two hours.

The Federal soldiers were massed forty columns deep. In fact, the whole force of the Yankee army was hurled against this point. No sooner would a regiment mount our works than they were shot down or surrendered. Yet still the Yankees came. It seemed impossible to check the onslaught. But every man was true to his trust. He seemed to think that at that moment the whole responsibility of the Confederate government rested upon his shoulders.

The sun beamed down on our uncovered heads, the thermometer being one hundred and ten degrees in the shade. A solid line of blazing fire right from the muzzles of the Yankee guns poured right into our very faces, singeing our hair and clothes. The hot blood of our dead and wounded spurted on us. The blinding smoke and stifling atmosphere filled our eyes and mouths. Afterward I heard a soldier say that he thought "Hell had broke loose in Georgia, sure enough."

I have heard men say that if they ever killed a Yankee during the war they were not aware of it. I am satisfied that on this memorable day, every man in our regiment killed from twenty to one hundred each. All that was necessary was to load and shoot.

When the Yankees fell back, and the firing ceased, I never saw so many broken down and exhausted men in my life. I was sick as a horse, and as wet with blood and sweat as I could be. Our tongues were parched and cracked for lack of water, and our faces blackened with powder and smoke. There was not a single man in the company who was not wounded, or had holes shot through his hat and clothing.

William A. Hughes, my old mess-mate and friend, was dead. I had just discharged the contents of my gun into the bosoms of two men, one right behind the other,

59

Reader, he died for me.

killing them both, and was reloading, when a Yankee rushed upon me and said, "You have killed my two brothers, and now I've got you." Everything I had ever done rushed through my mind. I heard the roar, and felt the flash of fire, and saw my more than friend, William A. Hughes, grab the muzzle of the gun, receiving the whole contents in his hand and arm, and mortally wounding him. Reader, he died for me. In saving my life, he lost his own.

Dead Angle was but a sample of others which followed each other in rapid succession. On the banks of the Chattahoochee River, a Yankee picket gave us the news: General Joseph E. Johnston had been removed, and General J. B. Hood appointed to take command.

The news came like a flash of lightning, staggering and blinding every one. It was like the successful gambler, flushed with continual winning, who staked his all and lost. It was like the end of the Southern Confederacy.

Atlanta

On the night of July 20th, 1864, the Yankees were on Peachtree Creek, advancing toward Atlanta. I was a picket that night, on the outpost of the army. When nearly day, I saw a man riding leisurely along on horseback. I soon saw that it was Mr. Mumford Smith, the old sheriff of Maury County. I was very glad to see him, and as soon as the relief guard came, I went back to camp with him. He brought a letter from home, from my father, and also a letter from "the gal I left behind me," enclosing a rosebud and two apple blossoms. I read that letter over five hundred times, and remember it today. I think I can repeat the poetry verbatim:

"I love you, O, how dearly,
    Words too faintly but express;
This heart beats too sincerely,
    E'er in life to love you less;
No, my fancy never ranges,
    Hopes like mine, can never soar;
If the love I cherish, changes,
    'Twill only be to love you more."

And then the letter wound up with, "May God shield and protect you, and prepare you for whatever is in store for you, is the sincere prayer of Jennie." You may be sure that I felt good and happy indeed.

On July 22, cannon balls, at long range, were falling

into the city of Atlanta. Details of citizens put out the fires as they would occur from the burning shells. We could see the smoke rise and hear the shells pass away over our heads as they went on toward the doomed city.

The plan of battle, as conceived and put into action by General Cleburne [a Confederate general], was one of the boldest conceptions and, at the same time, one of the most hazardous that ever occurred in our army during the war. The Yankees had fortified on two ranges of hills, leaving a gap in their breastworks in the valley entirely unfortified and unprotected. They felt that they could enfilade* the valley between the two lines so that no troop would or could attack at this weak point. General Walker, of Georgia, was ordered to attack on the extreme right. In the meantime, General Cleburne's division was marching by the right flank in a solid column, right up this valley, thus passing between the Yankee lines and cutting them in two.

The victory was complete. Large quantities of provisions and army stores were captured. The Federals had abandoned their entire line of breastworks. The battlefield was covered with their dead and wounded soldiers. I have never seen so many battle-flags left indiscriminately upon any battlefield. I ran over twenty in the charge, and could have picked them up everywhere. I did pick up one, and was promoted to Fourth Corporal for gallantry in picking up a flag on the battlefield.

As long as I was in action, fighting for my country, there was no chance for promotion. But as soon as I fell out

*enfilade — to rake with gunfire

THE CAMPAIGN AND SIEGE OF ATLANTA
MAY 1–SEPTEMBER 2, 1864

In spring 1864 General William Tecumseh Sherman and the Union Army were pushing toward Atlanta, Georgia, a major Confederate manufacturing and communications center. Confederate general Joseph Johnston planned to keep Sherman away from Atlanta as long as possible, at least until the presidential elections in November. Without a major Union victory, he reasoned, Northern voters might throw out Abraham Lincoln and elect a "pro-peace" candidate instead.

Sherman went after Johnston with everything he had, but Johnston kept avoiding a major engagement. During the Hundred Days' Battles, the armies had skirmished and withdrawn south down the railroad line to Atlanta. On June 27 at Kennesaw Mountain, the Union forces had launched a frontal assault up the mountain—at the Dead Angle. The Confederates withstood blistering fire and slaughtered more than two thousand Union soldiers. Southern losses were about four hundred.

Although the Confederates had won the day at Dead Angle, President Jefferson Davis continued to feel that Johnston fought too cautiously. Davis replaced him with John Bell Hood, a more aggressive but less skilled general. Hood attacked the enemy in battle on July 20, 22, and 28, but lost. The Army of Tennessee fell back behind Atlanta's defensive lines, and Sherman lay siege to the city. Confederate soldiers were finally evacuated on September 2, after Union forces seized the last rail connection to the city.

The Army of Tennessee—and Sam Watkins—slipped away to the north, where Hood planned to recover Tennessee for the Confederacy. Sherman and his 60,000 troops occupied Atlanta and then set off south on the famous March to the Sea, which sliced the Confederacy in two and cut a swath of destruction through Georgia.

of ranks and picked up a forsaken and deserted flag, I was promoted for it. Had I only known that picking up flags entitled me to promotion, and that every flag picked up would raise me one notch higher, I would have quit fighting and gone to picking up flags. By that means I would have soon been President of the Confederate States of America.

We went back to Atlanta. The old citizens had dug little cellars, which the soldiers called "gopher holes," and the women and children were crowded together in these cellars, while Sherman was trying to burn the city over their heads.

One day I thought I would visit the hospital. Great God! I get sick today when I think of all the agony, and suffering, and sickening stench, and odor of dead and dying. I cannot describe it. I remember I went in the rear of the building, and there I saw a pile of arms and legs, rotting and decomposing. I have no recollection in my whole life, of ever seeing anything that I remember with more horror than that pile of legs and arms.

Ah, reader, there is no glory for the private soldier, much less a conscript. The officers have all the glory. Glory is not for the private soldier, such as die in the hospitals, being eaten up with the deadly gangrene. Men who never fired a gun, or killed a Yankee during the whole war, are today the heroes of the war. Now, I tell you what I think about it: I think that those of us who fought as private soldiers, fought as much for glory as the Generals did, and those of us who stuck it out to the last, deserve more praise than the General who resigned because some other General was placed in command over him. A General could resign. That was honorable. A private could not resign, nor choose his branch of service, and if he deserted, it was death.

One morning about the break of day our artillery opened along our breastworks, scaring us almost to death, for it was the first guns that had been fired for more than a month. We were informed that they were "feeling" for the Yankees. The Yankees had gone—no one knew where—and our batteries were shelling the woods, feeling for them.

It turned out that the Yankees were twenty-five miles in our rear, "a hundred thousand strong," at a place called Jonesboro, and our corps had to go see about it.

On this day of which I now write we could see in plain view more than a thousand Yankee battle-flags waving on top the red earthworks, not more than four hundred yards off. Every private soldier there knew that General Hood's army was scattered all the way from Jonesboro to Atlanta, a distance of twenty-five miles, without any order, discipline, or spirit to do anything.

I have ever thought that Sherman was a poor general, not to have captured Hood and his whole army at that time. We had everything against us. The soldiers were broken down with their long days' hard marching—were almost dead with hunger and fatigue. Each one prayed that all this foolishness might end one way or the other. It was too much for human endurance. Every private soldier was willing to ring down the curtain, put out the footlights, and go home.

From this time until the close of the war, everything was a farce as to generalship. The tragedy had been played, the glory of war had departed.

General J. B. Hood established his headquarters at Palmetto, Georgia. At this place I was detailed as a regular scout. Our instructions were simply to try and find out all we could about the Yankees, and report all movements. I would go up to the Yankee outpost, and if some popinjay of a tacky officer didn't come along, we would have a good time. One morning I was sitting down to eat a good breakfast with the Yankee outpost. They were cavalry, and they were mighty clever and pleasant fellows. I looked down the road toward Atlanta, and not fifty yards from the outpost, I saw a body of infantry approaching.

Happening to catch sight of me, the captain asked, "What is this Rebel doing here?"

One of the men spoke up and tried to say something in my favor, but the more he said the more the captain would get mad. He started toward me two or three times. The cavalryman tried to protest, and said a few cuss words. The captain looked very mad at the cavalry. Here was my opportunity, now or never.

I took up my gun very gently and cocked it. I had the gentleman. When he turned to look again, it was a look of surprise. He was afraid to turn his head to give a command.

The cavalry motioned their hands at me, as much as to say, "Run, Johnny, run." I broke and ran like a quarter-horse.

One night five of us scouts put up at an old gentleman's

"What is this Rebel doing here?"

house. I took him for a Catholic priest. His head was shaved and he had on a loose gown like a lady's dress, and a large cord tied around his waist. A little while before day, the old priest came in and woke us up, and said he thought he saw a detachment of cavalry coming down the road toward the Rebel lines. I jumped up, put on one boot, and holding the other in my hand, I stepped out in the yard.

A Yankee captain stepped up to me and said, "Are you No. 200?" I answered huskily, "No, sir, I am not." He then went on in the house. I hallooed as loud as I could, "Look out, boys," and broke and ran. I had to jump over a garden picket fence, and as I lit on the other side, *Bang! Bang! Bang!* was fired right after me.

I had started back toward our lines, and had walked on about half a mile, when four Yankees jumped out in the middle of the road and said, "Halt there. Oh, yes, we've got you at last." I was in for it. If I started to run, I would be shot, so I surrendered.

I was taken prisoner. They, I thought, seemed very gleeful about it, and I had to march right back by the old priest's house. They carried me to a large, fine house, upstairs, and I was politely requested to take a seat. I sat there some moments, when a dandy-looking clerk of a fellow came up with a book in his hand, and said, "The name." I appeared not to understand, and he said, "The name." I still looked at him, and he said, "The name." Finally he closed the book with a slam and started off. Said I, "Did you want to find out my name?" He said, "I asked you three times." I said,

"When? If you ever asked me my name, I never heard it."
But he was too mad to listen to anything else.

I was carried to another room in the same building, and locked up. I remained there until about dark, when a man brought me a tolerably good supper, and then left me alone to my own meditations. I had made up my mind to escape, if there was any possible chance.

About 3 o'clock, everything got perfectly still. I took my knife and unscrewed the catch in which the lock was fastened, and soon found that I could open the door. I peeped down the stairs, and the guard was quietly walking to and fro on his beat. I made up my mind by his measured tread as to how often he would pass the door. One time, after he had just passed, I came out in the hall and started to run down the steps. About midway down the steps, one of them cracked very loud. But I ran on down in the lower hall and into a room, the door of which was open. The sentinel came back to the entrance of the hall, and listened a few minutes, and then moved on again.

I went to the window and raised the sash, but the blind was fastened with a kind of catch. I gave one or two hard pushes and felt it move. After that I made one big lunge, and it flew wide open. But it made a noise that woke up every sentinel. I jumped out into the yard and gained the street. On looking back, I heard the alarm given, and lights began to glimmer everywhere. I made tracks toward Peachtree Creek and went on until I made my way back to our lines.

Back to Tennessee

After remaining a good long time in Jonesboro, the news came that we were going to flank Atlanta. A flank means a "go around."

We passed around Atlanta, crossed the Chattahoochee, and traveled back over the same route on which we had made the arduous campaign under Joseph E. Johnston. We got back to Dalton, our starting point, [then to Tuscumbia, Alabama, and across the Tennessee River]. How every pulse did beat and leap, and how every heart did throb with joy, when we received the glad intelligence of our onward march toward the land of promise and our loved ones. Once more the Maury Grays were permitted to put their feet upon their native heath, and to revisit their homes and friends.

The Maury Grays left Columbia four years ago with 120 men. How many of those 120 original members are with the company today? Just twelve. We twelve will stick to our colors till she goes down forever, and until five more of this number fall dead and bleeding on the battlefield.

Kind reader, right here my pen, and my courage, and ability fail me. I shrink from butchery. Would to God I could tear the page from these memoirs and from my own memory. It is the blackest page in the history of the war of the Lost Cause. It was the finishing stroke to the independence of the Southern Confederacy.

Our regiment was resting in the gap of a range of hills in plain view of the city of Franklin. We could see the battle-flags of the enemy waving in the breeze. Our army had been depleted of its strength by a forced march from Spring Hill, and stragglers lined the road. Our artillery had not yet come up, and could not be brought into action. Our cavalry was across Harpeth River. Our army was but in a poor condition to make an assault.

While resting on this hillside, I saw a courier dash up to General, B. B. Cheatham. I knew then that we would soon be in action. Forward, march. We passed over the hill and through a little skirt of woods.

Right here in these woods, a detail of skirmishers was called for. If I had not been a skirmisher on that day, I would not have been writing this today.

As they marched on down through an open field, the Federal batteries began to open. A sheet of fire was poured into our very faces, and for a moment we halted as if in despair. Forward, men! Never on this earth did men fight against such terrible odds. Forward, men! It seemed that the very elements of heaven and earth were in one mighty uproar. Forward, men! And the blood spurted in a perfect jet from the dead and wounded.

But the skirmish line being deployed out, extending a little wider than the battle did—we advanced on toward the breastworks, on and on. I had made up my mind to die.

THE BATTLES OF FRANKLIN AND NASHVILLE

In fall 1864 General John Bell Hood still clung to the desperate hope that he could retake Tennessee. The first step was to capture Nashville, held by Federal troops. Hood, in constant pain from his wounds, recklessly ordered a frontal attack on Union forces at Franklin, just south of the city. He won a technical victory that came at a fearsome cost: more Southern officers were lost at Franklin than in any other conflict of the war.

After the battle Hood's forces were outnumbered two to one. At the Battle of Nashville, December 15–16, 1864, the Federals completed their destruction of his army. The Army of Tennessee was driven from the field, panicked and devastated. Humiliated, Hood asked to be relieved of command. In February 1865 Joseph E. Johnston took over again, only to surrender the army to General Sherman the following April.

It felt glorious. I passed on until I got to their works, walked up the ascent, and got over on the Yankees' side. I ran up on the line of works, where our men were engaged. Dead soldiers filled the entrenchments. The firing was kept up until midnight, and gradually died out. We passed the night where we were.

But when the sun began to light up the eastern sky, we looked over the battlefield. Oh, my God! What did we see? It was a grand holocaust of death. I never was so horrified and appalled in my life. Horses, like men, had died game on the gory breastworks. General Adams' horse had his forefeet on one side of the works and his hind feet on the other, dead. General Cleburne's mare had her forefeet on top of the works, dead in that position. General Cleburne's body was pierced with forty-nine bullets, through and through.

Four thousand five hundred privates! All lying side by side in death! Thirteen Generals were killed and wounded. I do not know who was to blame. It lives in the memory of the poor old Rebel soldier who went through that trying and terrible ordeal.

A few more scenes, and we close these memoirs. We marched toward the city of Nashville and bivouacked on the cold and hard-frozen ground. When we walked about, the echo of our footsteps sounded like the echo of a tombstone. The earth was crusted with snow, and the wind from the northwest pierced our very bones. A few raw-boned horses stood shivering under the ice-covered trees, nibbling on the short, scanty grass. Being in range of the Federal guns from Fort Negley, we were not allowed to have fires at night, and our thin and ragged blankets were but poor protection against the cold, raw blasts of December weather.

One morning about daylight our army began to move. The battle had begun. We were continually moving to our left. Our lines kept widening out, and stretching further and further apart, until there was not more than a skeleton of a skirmish line. We had to pass up a steep hill. Billy Carr and J. E. Jones and myself were the very extreme left wing of our army. I heard, "Surrender, surrender," and on looking around us, I saw that we were right in the midst of a Yankee line of battle. We immediately threw down our guns and surrendered.

J. E. Jones was killed at the first discharge of their guns. Another Yankee raised up and took deliberate aim at Billy Carr and fired. The ball struck him below the eye and passed through his head. I picked up my gun, and as the Yankee turned, I sent a minnie ball crushing through his head.

I broke and ran. A fallen dogwood tree tripped me up, and I fell over the log. It was all that saved me. Thousands of balls, it seemed to me, passed over it. As I got up to run again, I was shot through the middle finger of my hand and the thigh. How I got back I hardly know, for I was

He was very much agitated and affected, pulling his hair with his one hand and crying like his heart would break. I pitied him.

wounded and surrounded by Yankees. One rushed forward, and placing the muzzle of his gun within two feet of me, discharged it, but it missed its aim. I ran at him, grabbed him by the collar, and brought him off a prisoner. I had eight bullet holes in my coat and two in my hand, beside the one in my thigh and finger.

When I got back to where I could see our lines, it was one scene of confusion. Hood's army was routed and in full retreat.

I went to General Hood's headquarters. He was very much agitated and affected, pulling his hair with his one hand and crying like his heart would break. I pitied him, poor fellow. I asked him for a wounded furlough, and he gave it to me. I never saw him afterward. I always loved and honored him, and will ever revere and cherish his memory. He'd been shot in his legs and in one of his arms in the defense of his country at Gettysburg.* As a soldier, he was brave, good, noble, and gallant. But as a General he was a failure in every particular.

Our country was gone, our cause was lost.

*Hood lost the use of his arm as a result of his bravery at Gettysburg.

The Surrender

On the 10th of May, 1861, our regiment, the First Tennessee, left Nashville for the camp of instruction, with twelve hundred and fifty men, officers and line. Other recruits [and companies] made the sum total of 3,200 men that belonged to our regiment during the war.

Well, on the 26th day of April, 1865, General Joe E. Johnston surrendered his army at Greensboro, North Carolina. If I remember correctly, there were just sixty-five* men in all, including officers, that were released that day. Now, what became of the original 3,200? Reader, you may draw your own conclusions.

The day that we surrendered our regiment, it was a pitiful sight to behold. A mere squad of noble and brave men gathered around the tattered flag that they had followed in every battle through that long war. It was so bullet-riddled and torn that it was but a few blue and red shreds, that hung drooping while it, too, was stacked with our guns forever.

Our cause was lost from the beginning. Our greatest victories—Chickamauga and Franklin—were our greatest defeats. Our people were divided upon the question of union and secession. Our generals were scrambling for "Who ranked." The private soldier fought and starved and

*There were actually 125.

died for naught. Our hospitals were crowded with sick and wounded, but half provided with food and clothing to sustain life. Our money was depreciated to naught and our cause lost. The bones of our brave Southern boys lie scattered over our loved South. We love their memory yet.

When we pass away, the impartial historian will render a true verdict. History will then be written in justification and vindication of those brave and noble boys who gave their all in fighting the battles of their homes, their country, and their God.

The United States has no North, no South, no East, no West. *We are one and undivided.*

Time has brought many changes since I, a young, ardent, and impetuous youth, burning with a lofty patriotism, first shouldered my musket to defend the rights of my country.

Lifting the veil of the past, I see many manly forms, bright in youth and hope, standing in view by my side in Company H, First Tennessee Regiment. Before me, too, I see, not in imagination but in reality, my own loved Jennie, the partner of my joys and sharer of my sorrows.

The tale is told. The world moves on, the sun shines as brightly as before. The flowers bloom as beautifully, the birds sing their carols as sweetly, the trees nod and bow their leafy tops. The pale moon sheds her silvery sheen. The blue dome of the sky sparkles with trembling stars that twinkle and shine and make night beautiful, and the scene melts and gradually disappears forever.

The End

Editor's Note

Sam Watkins was a fine dramatic writer, and he told a good story. Occasionally he exaggerated or misremembered events, but scholars think that his account of life in the Army of Tennessee is on the whole accurate. The text in this book has been abridged and edited from a facsimile reprint of the 1900 edition of *"Co. Aytch": A Side Show of the Big Show.* (The text of the 1900 edition is identical to the first 1882 edition.)

In editing Sam's memoirs, I have often compressed or combined his sometimes long and ornate sentences. And where he slipped into present tense to give the effect of immediacy, I have changed the text back into past tense. Occasionally the punctuation has been modernized. Otherwise the wording is Watkins's throughout.

Glossary

amnesty pardon

artillery weapons, such as cannons, that discharge missiles; the unit of an army that fights with artillery

automaton robot

battery unit of four to six cannons in an artillery regiment

bayonet steel blade attached to a rifle and used in hand-to-hand combat

bivouac temporary camp

Bowie knife a kind of hunting knife

breastworks temporary defensive barriers made of earth, stone, or wood, standing breast high

caisson vehicle that carries artillery ammunition

camp of instruction training camp

cartridge a metal or paper tube containing powder and shot, which was inserted into the barrel of a rifle

cavalry soldiers mounted on horseback

chuck-a-luck a gambling game played with dice

cockade a rosette worn on a hat as a badge

colors identifying flag of an army unit or country

company the basic operational unit of the Civil War army, consisting of 30 to 125 men

conscript person who has been drafted into the military

countersign password

courier messenger

court-martial trial by military court

demoralize to upset and discourage

deployed placed in battle position

double quick to advance quickly

ensued followed

entrails internal organs

eschalots shallots (members of the onion family)

flank to attack from a vulnerable side; to go around

fortify to build defensive barriers

furlough a leave of absence granted to a soldier

holocaust total, fiery destruction

impregnable unconquerable

inextricable impossible to separate

infantry soldiers who fight on foot

Johnny Reb nickname for a Confederate soldier

minnie (minié) ball rifle bullet with a soft, cone-shaped head, which causes severe injuries

Napoleon gun twelve-pound brass cannon named after Napoleon III of France

picket line the outer perimeter of an army, patrolled by guards called pickets

popinjay self-important person

portent meaning or significance

ramrod a rod for pushing the cartridge into the barrel
    of a rifle

Rebels Confederates

recoil fall back under pressure

reconnoiter to explore an area to gain military information

regiment army unit consisting of ten companies

rhetoric the art of writing and public speaking

skirmish a minor fight in war; to scout around

Stars and Bars the first flag of the Confederacy

sutler merchant who sells provisions in an army camp

turbid stirred up and muddy

verbatim word for word

war of secession the Civil War

works defensive barriers made of wood, stone, or earth

yore time past

To Learn More about the Civil War

Books
Nonfiction

Corrick, James A. *Life among the Soldiers and Cavalry.*
San Diego: Lucent Books, 2000.

Hakim, Joy. *War, Terrible War.* A History of Us series.
New York: Oxford University Press, 1994.

Katcher, Philip. *The Civil War Source Book.* New York:
Facts on File, 1992.

McPherson, James M. *Fields of Fury: The Civil War.* New
York: Atheneum, 2002.

Murphy, Jim. *The Boys' War: Confederate and Union
Soldiers Talk About the Civil War.* New York: Clarion
Books, 1993.

Ray, Delia. *Behind the Blue and Gray: The Soldier's Life in
the Civil War.* New York: Puffin, 1996.

Reger, James P. *Life in the South during the Civil War.* San
Diego: Lucent Books, 1997.

Historical Fiction

Crane, Stephen. *The Red Badge of Courage.* New York:
Puffin, 1995.

Denenberg, Barry. *When Will This Cruel War Be Over? The Civil War Diary of Emma Simpson, Gordonsville, Virginia, 1864.* Dear America series. New York: Scholastic, 1996.

Fleishmann, Paul. *Bull Run.* New York: HarperTrophy, 1995.

Hunt, Irene. *Across Five Aprils.* New York: Berkeley, 1997.

Keith, Harold. *Rifles for Watie.* New York: HarperTrophy, 1991.

Lyons, Mary E., and Muriel Miller Branch. *Dear Ellen Bee: A Civil War Scrapbook of Two Union Spies.* New York: Atheneum, 2000.

Video and DVD

The Civil War: A Film by Ken Burns, 1990. PBS Home Video. The classic eleven-hour documentary.

Places to Visit

Atlanta Cyclorama, Atlanta, Georgia

Chickamauga and Chattanooga National Military Park, Fort Oglethorpe, Georgia

Kennesaw Mountain National Battlefield Park, Kennesaw, Georgia

Perryville Battlefield State Historic Site, Perryville, Kentucky

Pickett's Mill Historic Site, Dallas, Georgia

Manassas National Battlefield Park, Manassas, Virginia

Shiloh National Military Park, Shiloh, Tennessee

Websites*

The United States Civil War Center
www.cwc.lsu.edu
A comprehensive database of all topics related to the
   Civil War

National Park Service
www.nps.gov
Information on all National Parks and National
   Historical Parks with maps and activities

The American Civil War Homepage
Sunsite.utk.edu/civil-war/warweb.html
Offers a wealth of information, records, and resources on
   the Civil War

*Websites change from time to time. For additional on-line information, check
   with the media specialist at your local library.

Index

Page numbers for illustrations are in **boldface**

About the Editor

Ruth Ashby was educated at Yale University and the University of Virginia, where she taught women's studies and literature. She is the author of more than twenty books for young people, among them *Herstory* (Viking, 1995), *Elizabethan England* (Benchmark Books, 1999), *Victorian England* (Benchmark Books, 2003), and *Around the World in 1800* (Benchmark Books, 2003). She lives with her family on Long Island, New York, and teaches English at a nearby college when she is not writing and editing books.